The squadron emblems on *Triple Zilch* were 55th, 77th and 79th (front to rear) on both sides of the fuselage. Another aircraft equally as colorful was F-100D 55-3668 of which had previously served with the 55th squadron during 1957-58, during 1959 was to become the personal mount of Colonel J.T. Robbins who was deputy Wing Commander during April 1959, and took over command in July of that year.

He was assigned to the 55th and his aircraft bore the same design as *Triple Zilch* during this aircraft's 77th squadron assignment.

The emblem arrangement on 55-3668 was 77th, 55th and 79th from left to right on both sides of the fuselage.

In 1960 the markings changed once again and all squadrons had the fuselage streaks removed but retained the squadron emblems in their same position. The solid nose color gave way to a single nose band, a double nose band and three for a squadron commander.

F-100D, 56-3006 illustrated, is depicted with the three types of *Tiger* emblems in use by the 79th squadron during this period.

Triple Zilch had p- plied to nose and

During 1961 all ol- ors of a red, yellov er colors and embl m which was retain a change in the order of tail colors with blue, ye nt to rear. Other very colorful markings in the wing were applied when a team of F-100's were sent to Nellis Air Force Base, Nevada, to represent the USAFE at an annual gunnery meet. These comprised of triple colored nose bands fuselage and tail streak. Some known serials were 55-3665, 55-3666 and 55-3676, all bore the triple colors.

F-84G, 51-896, 77 Fighter Bomber Squadron, Wethersfield, Essex 1954. Streaks and bands are Red outlined in Black. Band across nose has worn off top. (Via G. Pennick)

F-84F, 52-6700 of the 77 Fighter Bomber Squadron, Squadron Commander's aircraft, all markings are Red and on the intake and exhaust the red is outlined in Black. Weathersfield AB, Essex 1957. (G. Pennick)

F-100D, 56-3000, 55 Tactical Fighter Squadron Commander's aircraft, *Triple Zilch* 1957 (USAF)

3

21st Fighter Bomber Wing

The 21st Fighter Bomber Wing was transferred from George AFB, California to various bases in France during 1954 to await the completion of Chambley AB. Markings on their F-86F Sabres consisted of painting the upper two thirds of the fin/rudder, minus the antenna cover with the squadron color. A tapered nose band was painted just forward of the gun ports and behind the intake ring, curving under the nose to include most of the larger nose landing gear door. All colored areas were bordered with very thin black striping and contained stars in a contrasting color. The 72 Fighter Bomber Squadron used red with white stars, the 416th used medium blue and white stars, while the 531st used yellow with black stars. There were at least two commander's aircraft with equal width starred red, yellow and blue horizontal (top to bottom) bands on the fin/rudder, but retaining the assigned squadron color on the nose. Sabre 25222 carried the red nose markings of the 72 Fighter Bomber Squadronas well as a multi colored band around the fuselage, just behind the wing, of yellow, red, blue, and yellow with each color bordered in white. A personal insignia of a helmeted rat sitting at a desk was on the left side of the fuselage, just under the cockpit. The other commanders aircraft was 31147, which had its fin/rudder painted identical to 222, but had a yellow nose for the 531 Fighter Bomber Squadron, fuselage bands or insignia. As of this writing, no 21 Fighter Bomber Wing Sabre is known to have carried either wing or squadron insignia.

These markings were used until the deactivation of the 21 FBW in late 1957 at which time the Sabres were handed over to various NATO countries.

36 · Fighter Bomber Group

Squadron Colors   22 FBS Red   23 FBS Blue   53 FBS Green

The 36th Fighter Bomber Group with three squadrons of F-80Bs, the 22, 23 and 53 Fighter Bomber Squadron, moved from Panama to Furstenfeldbruck A.B. Germany during 1948 via an aircraft carrier. These aircraft were in natural metal finish and did not even carry buzz numbers (FT followed by the last three of the serial) as most other F-80s in the USAF did at that time. The Group marking consisted of a thin jagged lightning streak with a diamond shaped head foremost.

These designs were painted in the appropriate squadron colors, with the 22 FBS being Red, 23 FBS Blue and 53 FBS Green.

The aircraft also had the same color band on the fin and rudder, just under the antenna cover. All aircraft carried a unit ID number on their noses, with numbers 1-9 for the HQ squadron, 10-39 for the 22 FBS, 40-69 for the 23 FBS and 70-99 for the 53 FBS, painted in the squadron color. The ID numbers were removed during 1949, and buzz numbers painted on the fuselages, above the wing and on the noses in black.

The *Skyblazers* Aerobatic Team was formed about this time and four F-80s had this name painted on both sides of the nose.

In late 1950, the 36th Group began to re-equip with the F-84E, having been ferried across to Germany by the 27 Fighter Escort Group. The first markings carried by the F-84Es of the 36 FBG, appear to have been geometric designs with a single capital letter inside, painted on the tails. It is believed that the shape of these designs indicated the squadron assigned. A solid color circle with a light colored 'J' was painted on 49-2293, while aircraft with letters inside squares included, 92199/V, 92200/Z, 92304/D and 92313/P. It is believed that the geometric designs for each of the squadrons was as follows; 22 FBS a Diamond, 23 FBS a Circle and 53 FBS a Square.

In 1951 the markings became more elaborate with all of the F-84 tail surfaces being painted in light blue and White stripes, angled up to the vertical surfaces and out on the horizontal surfaces about 15 degrees. Squadron colors were painted on the tip tanks and around the nose, forward of the buzz numbers and including the front of the nose wheel doors. Tip tanks had the same streak design on the outside as used on the F-80s. The 22 FBS used red with white trim, the 23rd medium Blue with White, and 53 FBS Yellow and Black. Squadron badges were painted on the left side of the fuselage just above the wing's leading edge and the Group emblem in the same position on the right side. The 22 FBS continued the *Skyblazers* Aerobatic Team using four of their normal marked aircraft and performing exciting displays from Europe and North Africa to their last show at Detroit in August 1952.

Some F-84s carried non standard markings such as Wing Commander Colonel Robert L. Scott's 92299 with *Flying Tiger* markings as his personal markings, for he once commanded the 23 Tactical Fighter Wing whose emblems were on his F-84. This aircraft had a Gold streak on the tip tanks and four Blue or Black bands around the fuselage.

Another aircraft had white tip tanks, while still another had Bronze colored tanks with Green and White trim, and a Red, White and Blue intake band.

36 Fighter Day Wing

Squadron Colors   22 FDS *Red*   23 FDS *Medium Blue*
53 FDS Yellow   32 FDS *Green*   461 FDS *Black*

In 1953 F-86Fs started to arrive, replacing the F-84Es. In 1955 the 36th became known as the Fighter Day Wing, and had five squadrons assigned to it, the 22, 23, 53, and the two new ones, the 32 Fighter Day Squadron at Soesterberg, Netherlands and the 461st FDS (Ex-527 FDS) at Hahn.

At first the markings consisted of a Korean Theatre styled Yellow and Black bordered fuselage band just behind the wing. This gave way to a new style of marking where the whole group adopted three wide angled bands on the upper part of the fin and rudder, angled down on the forward end. These were painted in individual squadron colors often with white or black trim lines.

The 22 FBS continued using Red, 23 FBS used medium Blue, the 53 FBS Yellow, 32 Green and 461 Black.

The F-86Fs of the 461 FDS, at one stage in their markings history carried their squadron badge on both sides of the tail with Black bands containing Yellow diamonds.

36th Tactical Fighter Wing F-100C

By June 1956, the F100C Super Sabre was being flown by the 23 and 53 squadrons and shortly afterwards all five squadrons were operating this aircraft.

The markings consisted of the three diagonal tail stripes with appropriate colored trim lines throughout, and the noses received colors also.

The *Arrowheads* painted below the cockpit contained pilots and crew chiefs names, while squadron emblems were positioned on both sides of fuselage on the ammo doors, the exception being F100C 54-1996 of which was the Commanders aircraft and this bore wing emblems.

The *Skyblazer's* aerobatic team was reformed, having previously been taken over by the 48th Tactical Fighter Wing, flying F-86Fs. The F100Cs were painted in the striking Red, White and Blue markings, drop tanks were not normally carried during displays but were added near the end of the teams era.

The *Skyblazers* emblem was carried on the left side of fuselage and USAFE one on the right.

F100C 54-2009 was a lead aircraft and bore a sloping Red, White and Blue fuselage band just behind the national insignia on the rear fuselage. Various aircraft have operated with the *Skyblazers* and some of the known serial numbers are: 54-1959, 54-1980 and 54-2010. The team was disbanded in January 1962.

The 32nd Squadron was based at Soesterberg in the Netherlands and came under direct Dutch control, so the green markings gave way to the Red, White and Blue of the National flag, this took place during late 1958.

The 461 FDS disbanded in 1959, and the 32 FDS transferred to the 86 Fighter Interceptor Wing in 1960 and became the 32 Fighter Interceptor Squadron flying the F102 Delta Dart.

The F105 Thunder Chief started to re-equip the 36 Tactical Fighter Wing in 1961, and at this time the wing reverted to the three original squadrons keeping their same colors as previously used on the F100s. 22TFS Red, 23TFS Blue, 53TFS Yellow.

The diagonal band markings were painted on at the Brookley AFB Depot in Alabama, prior to the delivery flight, and so arrived at Bitburg in full colors. The 36 Wing Commander's aircraft, serial No. 60-0436 had its three stripes in Red, Blue and Yellow from top to bottom. By late 1962, a change took place whereby all F105s of the 36TFW had the triple colored bands as there were no more squadron assigned aircraft. This scheme remained until the advent of camouflage to the wing in 1965.

F-105D, 60-432, 22 Tactical Fighter Squadron, 36 Tactical Fighter Wing photographed in the Summer of 1961. Tail bands Red edged in White. (D MENARD)

F-84E's of the 22 Fighter Bomber Squadron, 36 Fighter Bomber Group, *Skyblazers***, from Furstenfeldbruck AB Germany in 1951 carry red intake band and drop tanks. Tail stripes are blue and white.**

F-100C, 54-2010 of the *Skyblazers* **seen at Hahn AB, Germany 1961-62 (D MENARD)**

F-100C, 54-1865, 23 Tactical Fighter Squadron, 36 Tactical Fighter Wing at Furstenfeldbruck 1956. Markings are light blue with white trim. 23 Tactical Fighter Squadron Emblem on fuselage. (G JOOS)

F-86F, 53-1192 in the later *Skyblazer* scheme adopted by the Team. Chaumont AB, France 1956. (USAF)

48 Fighter Bomber Wing

Squadron Colors   492 FBS   Medium Blue and White
493 FBS   Yellow and Medium Blue   494 FBS   None

The F-84G equipped the 48 Fighter-Bomber wing and was activated at Chaumont A.B., France in 1952.

Colors applied to the 492 FBS comprised of medium Blue and White bands around the nose back to the front part of the nose wheel doors, Blue and White bands around front of tip tanks and vertical bands on the tail surface.

The 493 FBS used Yellow and Medium Blue in the form of Yellow tip tanks and tail with a Blue streak superimposed on both.

The 494 FBS did not carry any distinctive markings on their aircraft although quite a number of 48th wing aircraft were to be seen in an experimental camouflage consisting of Grey, Brown and Blue, retaining the large National insignia.

With the introduction of the F-86F to the wing in 1953, the aircraft first carried solid colors on all tail surfaces including dorsal fins in the appropriate assigned squadron color, the 492 FBS medium Blue, 493 FBS yellow and 494 FBS red. These colors were to remain with each squadron throughout their careers. By mid 1954, squadron emblems had begun to appear on both sides of the fuselage just over the wing. It is believed that there were no significant changes in the F86F markings, however, F-86F 53-1222 became 494 Squadron Commander's aircraft and bore three Red fuselage bands with the squadron emblem on the fuselage and a torch and flame design on the tail.

A T-33 was also seen in the same style markings but in triple colors. During 1954, the *Skyblazers* were taken over by the 48 FBW and their F-86Fs adorned in a Red, White and Blue scheme. The first design used comprised of the tail surfaces and outer wing panels being painted with large areas of Red and White with various sized medium Blue stars in the White areas.

The second design, in 1956, had Blue on all tail surfaces and outer wing panels and placed White stars in the Blue area. The *Skyblazer* legend was painted on in Red in old english script, and the *Statue De La Liberty* emblem was on both sides of the fuselage.

48th Tactical Fighter Wing F-100D/F

The F-100D Super Sabre entered into service with the 48th Fighter Bomber Wing during 1956 and the unit was redesignated 48 Tactical Fighter Wing. These aircraft were the 1954 models and in time were replaced by the 1956 version.

The first markings applied were in the form of the center tail section being painted in the individual squadron colors, while aircraft number 54-2222 became the Commanders and bore the triple colors, one for each of his squadrons. The Wing emblem was positioned on both sides of the nose section on his aircraft while squadron machines had the squadron emblem on the left and wing emblem on the right.

With the introduction of the later model F-100D, the markings were changes and consisted of stripes running from the nose to tail and on the ends of the wings, in appropriate squadron colors, except for 56-3262 which became the Commander's aircraft for a while. The Commander was Colonel Stanton Smith and for his aircraft, triple colored stripes were adopted.

The emblems remained in the same way as on the 1954 Sabre variant except that they were placed slightly lower down on the fuselage and had White trails radiating from them, containing the pilot's name on the left and crew chief's on the right.

Autumn 1959 saw another change in the design whereupon the nose stripes were painted over and a Vee being added to the nose section.

Early in January 1960, the 48th wing left Chaumont Air Base and proceeded to take up residence at Lakenheath, Suffolk, when, shortly after this, the markings went through another change. This time the tail bands were removed and an Alar was applied, wing stripes were also removed and replaced by a single one in appropriate squadron color.

The markings remained this way until 1962 when the final change took place, whereupon all aircraft of the wing bore the triple colors on nose and tail with triple colored bands painted on the ends of the wings. The 48th wing emblem positioned behind the Alar on both sides of the tail.

In 1964, the wing emblem was changed to a smaller shield design but still bearing the *Statue De La Liberte* motto bestowed on the 48th wing when in France, thus making it the only USAF Unit to officially bear a numerical and descriptive title. The wing bands were also removed but the wing fences were painted yellow.

F-86F, 53-1180 of the 48 Fighter Bomber Wing. Squadron allocation and colors are unknown. C. 1954-55. (MAP)

F-86F, 53-1201 of the 48 Fighter Bomber Wing *Skyblazers* **in the early scheme used by the Team. 1955 (MAP)**

F-100D, 56-3288 in the yellow tail and intake markings of the 493 Tactical Fighter Squadron at Toul-Rosieres AB, France 1959. (D MENARD)

F-100D, 56-3262 of the 494 Tactical Fighter Squadron also at Toul-Rosieres, France 1959. Tail stripes and nose alar are in the squadron color-Red. (D MENARD)

56-3288 in revised markings of the 493 Tactical Fighter Squadron, at Waddington's Battle of Britain Display. A Yellow alar is carried at both the nose and tail position. September 1961. (MAP)

49th Tactical Fighter Wing

Squadron Colors   *7 TFS* *Blue*
8 TFS *Yellow*   *9 TFS* *Red*

F-100D Super Sabre

The 388 tactical fighter wing was based in Europe from 1954 until December, 1957, during which time the wing operated the F86F and F86H Sabre until late 1956 when the Sabres were replaced by the F-100D/F.

In December, 1957, the 388th TFW reformed in the United States but its F-100s remained in Europe, on this same day the 49th Tactical Fighter Wing was formed and took over the F-100s in the squadron markings adopted by the former unit.

The 49th Tactical Fighter Wing comprised of three squadrons, number 7, 8 and 9 with each carrying an individual color on the aircraft's nose and tail with a lightning streak superimposed on the tail. Colors were: No. 7 squadron, light Blue with a White streak, No. 8 squadron, Yellow with a Black streak, No. 9, Red with a White streak.

Squadron emblems were not always carried although one or two aircraft could be seen with one positioned on either side of the nose just below the front part of the cockpit.

The 49th wing was based at Etain/Rouvres, France but moved to Spangdahlem, Germany during 1959, and in early 1960, a change was made in the markings whereby all aircraft were painted in the triple colors on nose and tail. The markings remained this way until the wing converted to the F-105 Thunderchief in 1962.

49th Tactical Fighter Wing
F-105D/F Thunderchief

The F-105 commenced service with the 49th Tactical Fighter Wing during 1962.

The broad tail band colors and streak, previously carried on the F-100 were deleted in favor of a triple colored wing design with the 49th wing emblem in the base and on both sides of the tail. A triple colored streak was also carried on both sides of the nose while nose wheel doors were painted in the individual squadron color, which re-

mained the same for each squadron as in the F-100 era.

Some examples being: F-105D, 61-0100 of the 9th squadron with Red nose wheel doors and 61-0111 with dark Blue of the 7th squadron. Some colorful F-105F's were 63-8311 of the 8th squadron, this aircraft lacked the nose streak but not only had yellow nose wheel doors, it also had yellow main under carriage doors. F-105F, 63-8300 was exactly the same but bore Red for the 9th squadron.

Squadron emblems were not always carried, and some aircraft carried them on the lower fuselage sides. The markings remained this way until the advent of camouflage in 1965 and the F-105s later went to Vietnam.

F-100D, 56-3300, 7 Tactical Fighter Squadron, 49 Tactical Fighter Wing, Toul-Rosieres, France 1959. Markings are light Blue and White. (D MENARD)

50th Tactical Fighter Wing
F86F - F86H

The 50th fighter bomber wing, as it was then titled, was comprised of three squadrons. The squadrons and their colors were: 10th Blue, 81st Yellow and the 417th Red.

In 1953 the wing equipped with F-86F Sabre and one of the earliest schemes to be seen, comprised a Yellow band edged in Black on the fuselage and tail and a Yellow nose band with black stars, as seen on aircraft 52-4724 which served with the 81st squadron. The 81 squadron emblem appeared on both sides of the tail and the wing emblem was on both sides of the fuselage.

A short time later, the markings became more standard, with aircraft having bands of individual squadron colors painted on the nose and tail containing appropriate colored stars. Squadron emblems were painted on both sides of the tail.

F-86H, 53-1433, 10 Tactical Fighter Squadron, 50 Tactical Fighter Wing. Light Blue and White markings with 10th Squadron Badge on tail. 1956. (MAP)

F-100D, 55-2934, 81 Tactical Fighter Squadron, 50 Tactical Fighter Wing at Toul-Rosieres, France, June 1959. (D MENARD)

F-100D, 56-3227 of the 50 Tactical Fighter Wing, note the Red and White 417 Tactical Fighter Squadron markings on nose wheel door and drop tanks, Lakenheath AB, 1965. (MAP)

In 1955, some F86Fs from the 50th TFW were selected to represent the USAF in Europe at an annual weapons meet at Nellis Air Force Base, for this the aircraft were painted in triple colored markings with the Wing emblem on each side of the tail.

Later in the year, the 50th wing began to re-equip with the F-86H-10-NH version of the Sabre armed with four 20mm cannons. This was one of only two units in Europe to operate this aircraft and although the markings remained the same as on the F-86F, the squadron emblems were considerably larger. During 1956, a new Wing emblem was approved and for a short time both the old and new type were in use.

The Commander of the 50th Wing, flew F-86H 53-1500 with the triple colors on his aircraft, with the serial number in White except for the 50 with a small *th* above it and the buzz number painted in black with the same 50th application. The new Wing emblem was positioned on both sides of the fuselage.

50th Tactical Fighter Wing
F-100D/F

The F-100 and F Super Sabre entered service with the Wing during 1958. Markings of all squadrons continued in the same way as applied to the F Sabres.

An F-100F, 56-3847 was the 417th Squadron Commander's aircraft and had three Red tail bands with the 417th emblem superimposed on the center one with a star in front and two behind the emblem.

Other markings were Pilot's wings below the left side of the cockpit containing the pilot's name and a double ended wrench was painted on the right side with the crew chief's name in it.

Drop tanks also had the fins painted in the squadron color with a star on the outer fin.

Colonel C. Banbury who commanded the Wing, was assigned to the 81st squadron in 1958. He flew F-100D, 55-2950 and this aircraft bore the triple colors of the Wing with the Wing emblem on both sides of the tail. The wing tips were painted Yellow for the 81st squadron while the buzz number on the fuselage was represented in a different way, the number nine in White and a large *TH* above the fifty. This particular aircraft was lost during the latter part of 1960 but the pilot was unhurt.

Shortly after this, F-100F, 56-3830 was assigned to the same squadron, having previously carried the predominantly Yellow markings of the 81st Squadron, it was now to be seen with the same markings as 55-2950 except that the serial number on the fuselage was standard.

In 1960, the individual squadron colors were removed from all 50th Wing aircraft and replaced by the triple colors on the tail with appropriate White and Black trim lines. The 50th wing emblem was superimposed in the Yellow stripe on both sides of the tail. Drop tanks were still to be seen painted as in 1958/59.

These markings remained in use until 1965, when camouflage covered all.

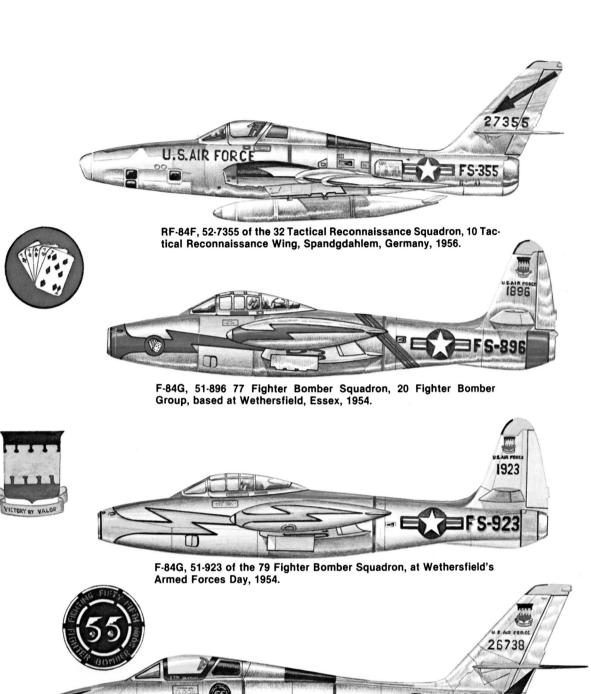

RF-84F, 52-7355 of the 32 Tactical Reconnaissance Squadron, 10 Tactical Reconnaissance Wing, Spandgdahlem, Germany, 1956.

F-84G, 51-896 77 Fighter Bomber Squadron, 20 Fighter Bomber Group, based at Wethersfield, Essex, 1954.

F-84G, 51-923 of the 79 Fighter Bomber Squadron, at Wethersfield's Armed Forces Day, 1954.

F-84F, 52-6738 55 Fighter Bomber Squadron, based at Wethersfield, 1956.

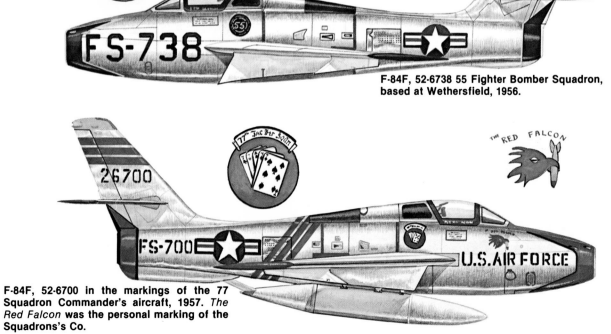

THE RED FALCON

F-84F, 52-6700 in the markings of the 77 Squadron Commander's aircraft, 1957. *The Red Falcon* was the personal marking of the Squadrons's Co.

F-84F, 52-6539 of the 79 *Tiger* Squadron based at Woodbridge, Suffolk, 1957.

F-100D, 55-3668 of the 55 Tactical Fighter Squadron, at Wethersfield, Essex, August 1958.

F-100D, 55-3668 re-painted as Deputy Commanders aircraft, assigned to the 55 Tactical Fighter Squadron, Wethersfield, May 1959.

F-100D, 56-3000 20 Tactical Fighter Wing Commander's aircraft, assigned to the 55th Squadron, 1957.

Triple Zilch 20 Wing Commander's aircraft assigned to the 77th Squadron at Wethersfield, Essex, 1958.

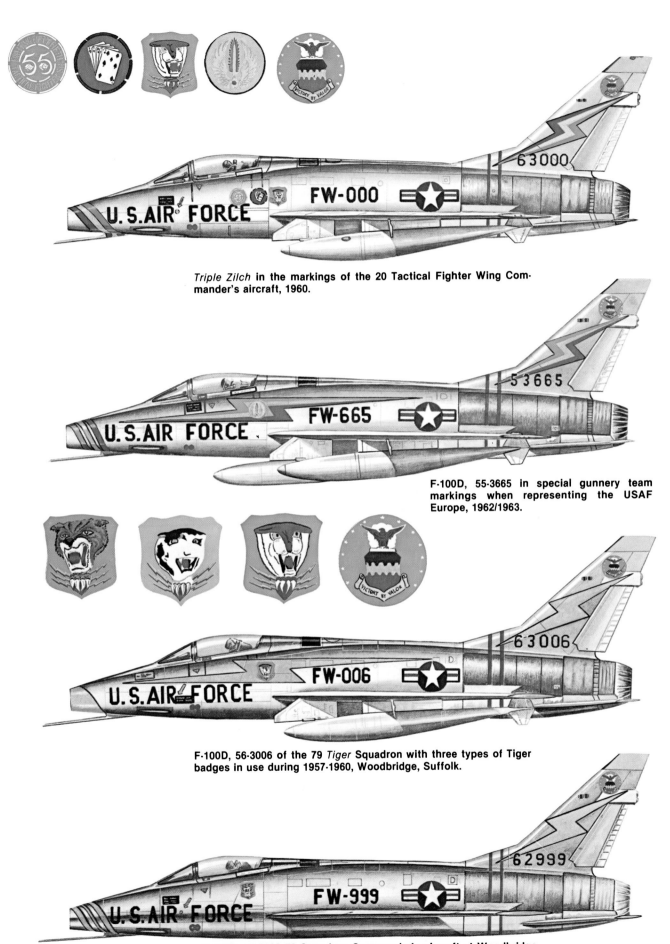

Triple Zilch in the markings of the 20 Tactical Fighter Wing Commander's aircraft, 1960.

F-100D, 55-3665 in special gunnery team markings when representing the USAF Europe, 1962/1963.

F-100D, 56-3006 of the 79 *Tiger* Squadron with three types of Tiger badges in use during 1957-1960, Woodbridge, Suffolk.

F-100D, 56-2999 79 Squadron Commander's aircraft at Woodbridge, Suffolk, 1960.

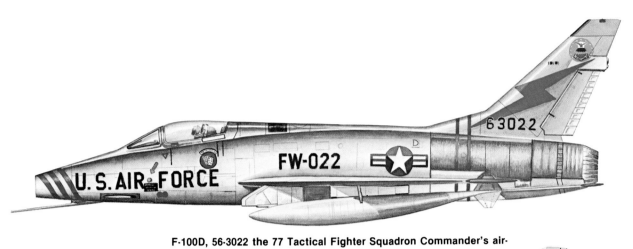

F-100D, 56-3022 the 77 Tactical Fighter Squadron Commander's aircraft, 1960.

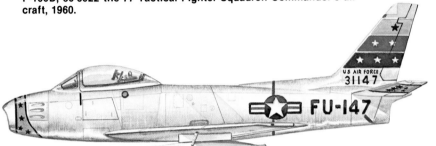

F-86F, 53-1147 of the 531 Fighter Bomber Squadron, 21st Fighter Bomber Wing, Wing Commander's aircraft at Wheelus A.B., Lybia, June 1956.

F-86F, 53-1147, 531 Squadron Commander's aircraft based at Chambley, France, 1957.

F-86F, 52-5222, 21 Fighter Bomber Wing Commander's aircraft, 1957.

F-80B, 45-8598, 36 Fighter Group Commander's aircraft at Furstenfeldbruch, Germany, 1949.

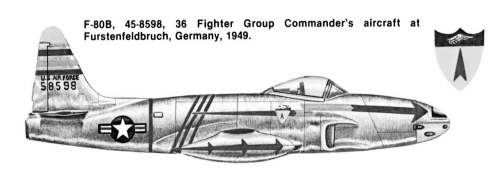

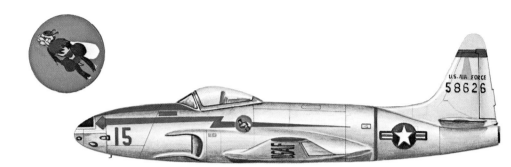

F-80B, 45-8626, 22 Fighter Bomber Squadron, 36 Fighter Group, 1949.

F-84E, 49-2229, of the 22 Fighter Bomber Squadron, 36 Fighter Bomber Group, in markings adopted during 1950.

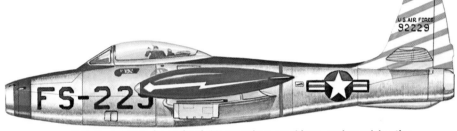

F-84E, 49-2229, in revised 22 squadron markings and used by the *Skyblazers,* 1951.

F-84E, 49-2299, 36 Fighter Bomber Wing Commander Colonel Robert L. Scott's aircraft, Furstenfeldbruch, Germany, 1952.

F-84E, 49-2166 of the 23 Fighter Bomber Squadron.

F-84E, 49-2189 of the 53 Fighter Bomber Squadron at Bitburg A.B., Germany, 1953.

F-86F, 52-5423 of the 461 Fighter Day Squadron, (Ex.527FBS) 36th Fighter Day Group, based at Hahn, Germany, 1956.

F-100C, 54-2010 of the *Skyblazers* Aerobatic Team (36 Tactical Fighter Wing) Bitburg A.B., Germany, 1961.

F-100C, 54-1996 36 Tactical Fighter Wing Commander's aircraft, based at Bitburg, 1958.

F-100C, 54-2007 of the 53 *Bitburg Tigers* Squadron, 1959.

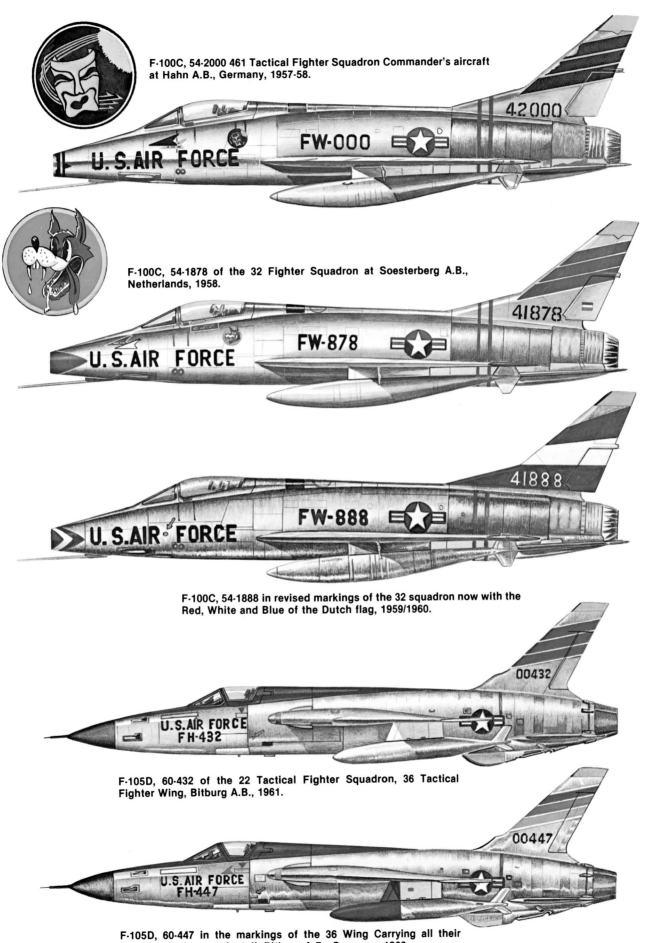

F-100C, 54-2000 461 Tactical Fighter Squadron Commander's aircraft at Hahn A.B., Germany, 1957-58.

F-100C, 54-1878 of the 32 Fighter Squadron at Soesterberg A.B., Netherlands, 1958.

F-100C, 54-1888 in revised markings of the 32 squadron now with the Red, White and Blue of the Dutch flag, 1959/1960.

F-105D, 60-432 of the 22 Tactical Fighter Squadron, 36 Tactical Fighter Wing, Bitburg A.B., 1961.

F-105D, 60-447 in the markings of the 36 Wing Carrying all their Squadron colors on the tail, Bitburg A.B., Germany, 1962.

F-84G, 51-868 493 Fighter Bomber Squadron, 48 Fighter Bomber Group, Chaumont A.B., France, 1952.

F-86F, 53-1192 of the *Skyblazers* of the 48 Tactical Fighter Wing, Chaumont, A.B., France, 1955.

F-86F, 53-1192 in the later scheme adopted by the *Skyblazers* of the 48 Tactical Fighter Wing, Chaumont, France, 1956.

F-100D, 54-2222 flown by Colonel Stanton T. Smith Jr., the 48th Tactical Fighter Wing Commander, Chaumont A.B., France, 1956.

F-100D, 56-3262 48 Tactical Fighter Wing Commander, Colonel Smith's aircraft in gunnery team markings at William Tell, 1958.

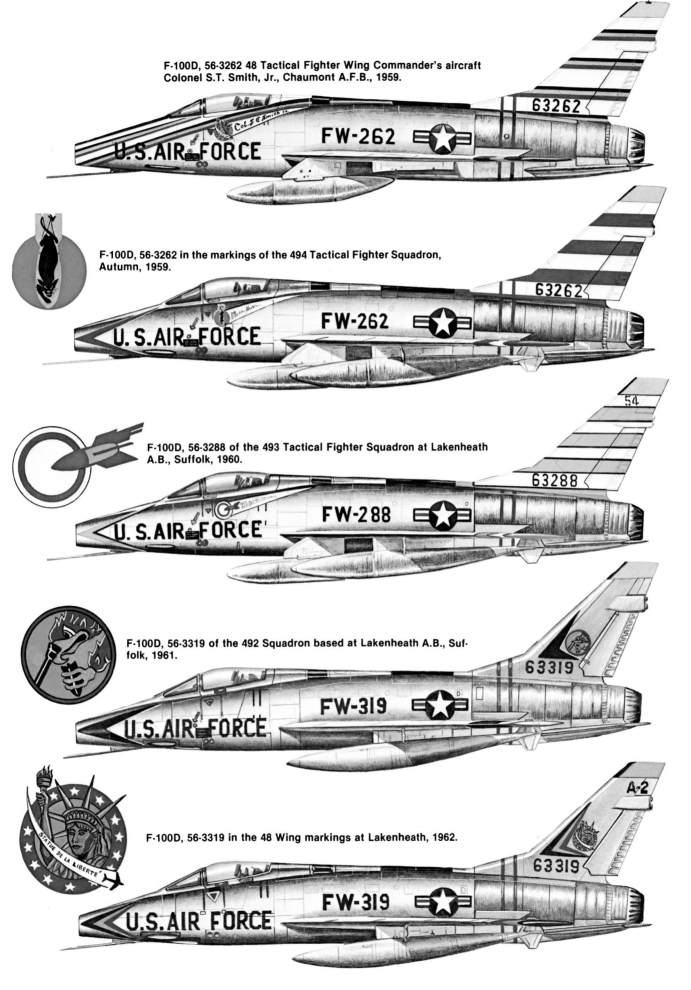

F-100D, 56-3262 48 Tactical Fighter Wing Commander's aircraft
Colonel S.T. Smith, Jr., Chaumont A.F.B., 1959.

F-100D, 56-3262 in the markings of the 494 Tactical Fighter Squadron,
Autumn, 1959.

F-100D, 56-3288 of the 493 Tactical Fighter Squadron at Lakenheath
A.B., Suffolk, 1960.

F-100D, 56-3319 of the 492 Squadron based at Lakenheath A.B., Suffolk, 1961.

F-100D, 56-3319 in the 48 Wing markings at Lakenheath, 1962.

F-100D, 56-3206 8 Tactical Fighter Squadron of the 49th Tactical Fighter Wing, Spangdahlem, Germany, 1959.

F-100D, 55-3691 in the 49 Tactical Fighter Wing Commander's markings at Spangdahlem, 1960.

F-105D, 61-094, 8 Tactical Fighter Squadron of the 49 Tactical Fighter Wing, Spangdahlem A.B., Germany, 1965.

F-86F, 52-4724 of the 81 Fighter Bomber Squadron, 50th Fighter Bomber Wing at Hahn A.B., Germany, 1954-55.

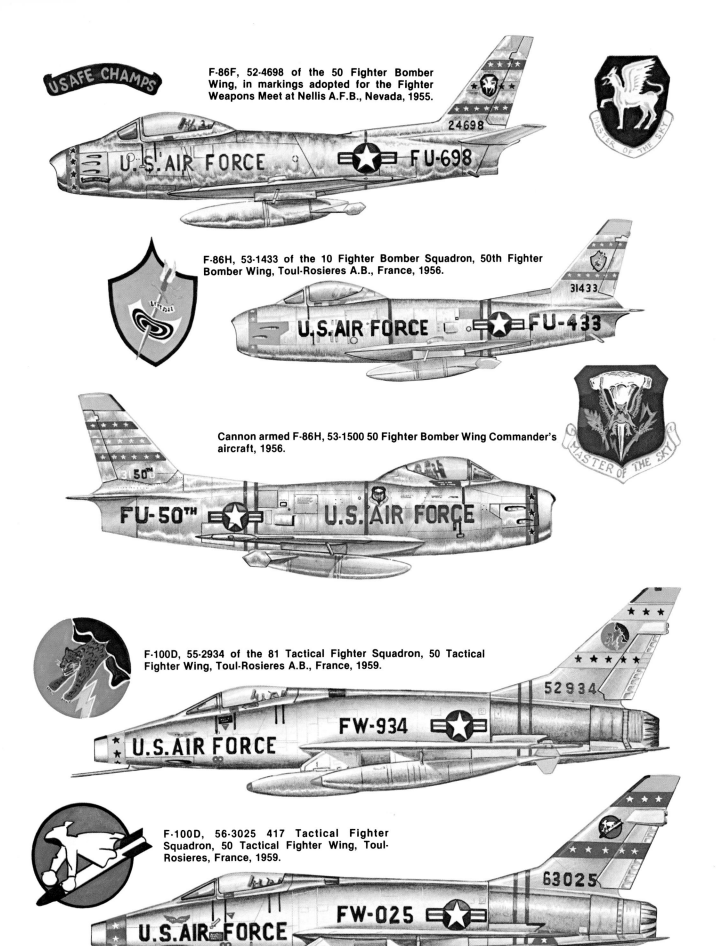

USAFE CHAMPS

F-86F, 52-4698 of the 50 Fighter Bomber Wing, in markings adopted for the Fighter Weapons Meet at Nellis A.F.B., Nevada, 1955.

F-86H, 53-1433 of the 10 Fighter Bomber Squadron, 50th Fighter Bomber Wing, Toul-Rosieres A.B., France, 1956.

Cannon armed F-86H, 53-1500 50 Fighter Bomber Wing Commander's aircraft, 1956.

F-100D, 55-2934 of the 81 Tactical Fighter Squadron, 50 Tactical Fighter Wing, Toul-Rosieres A.B., France, 1959.

F-100D, 56-3025 417 Tactical Fighter Squadron, 50 Tactical Fighter Wing, Toul-Rosieres, France, 1959.

19

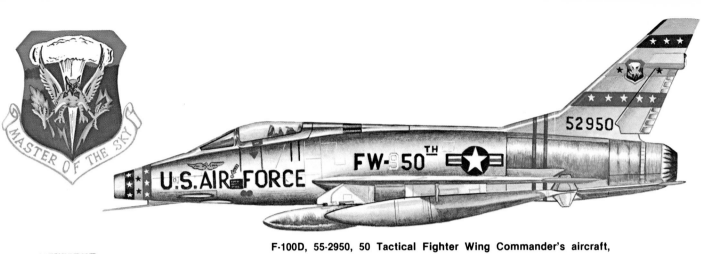

F-100D, 55-2950, 50 Tactical Fighter Wing Commander's aircraft, 1958.

RF-84F, 52-7343, 66 Tactical Reconnaissance Wing Commander's aircraft as seen at Wethersfield's Armed Forces Day, Essex, 1957.

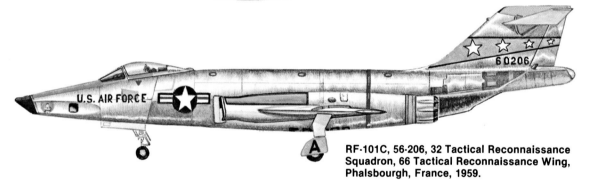

RF-101C, 56-206, 32 Tactical Reconnaissance Squadron, 66 Tactical Reconnaissance Wing, Phalsbourgh, France, 1959.

66 TRW

17 TRS

18 TRS

32 TRS

38 TRS

RF-101C, 56-089 of the 38 Tactical Reconnaissance Squadron, 1959-60.

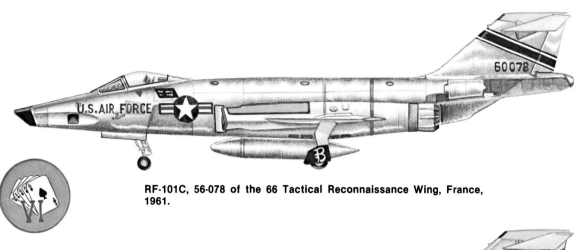

RF-101C, 56-078 of the 66 Tactical Reconnaissance Wing, France, 1961.

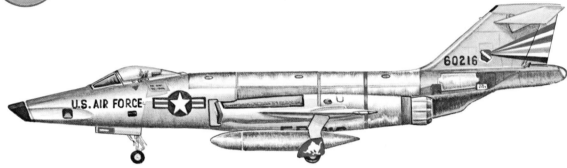

RF-101C, 56-216, 17 Tactical Reconnaissance Squadron, 66 Tactical Reconnaissance Wing in final markings, 1963.

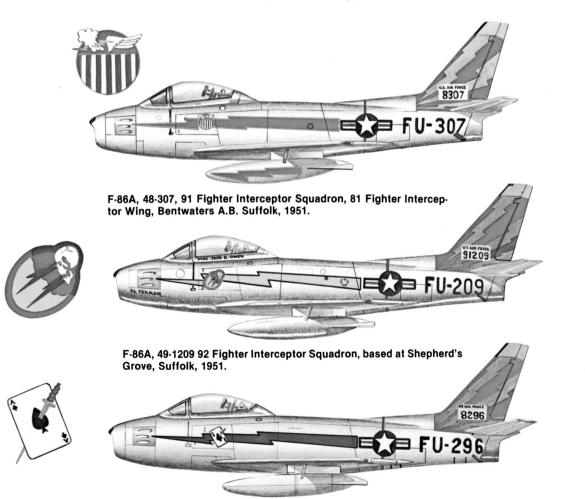

F-86A, 48-307, 91 Fighter Interceptor Squadron, 81 Fighter Interceptor Wing, Bentwaters A.B. Suffolk, 1951.

F-86A, 49-1209 92 Fighter Interceptor Squadron, based at Shepherd's Grove, Suffolk, 1951.

F-86A, 48-296 of the 116 Fighter Interceptor Squadron, Shepherd's Grove, 1951.

F-84F, 52-6780, 78 Fighter Bomber Squadron, 81st Fighter Bomber
Wing, based at Shepherd's Grove, Suffolk, 1958.

F-84F, 52-6675, 78 Squadron Commander's aircraft, 1958.

F-84F, 52-6834 of the 91 Fighter Bomber Squadron, 81 Fighter
Bomber Wing, Squadron Commander's aircraft, Lt. Colonel
Moreland, Bentwaters A.B., Suffolk, 1958.

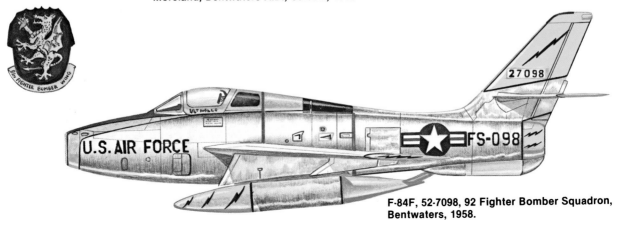

F-84F, 52-7098, 92 Fighter Bomber Squadron,
Bentwaters, 1958.

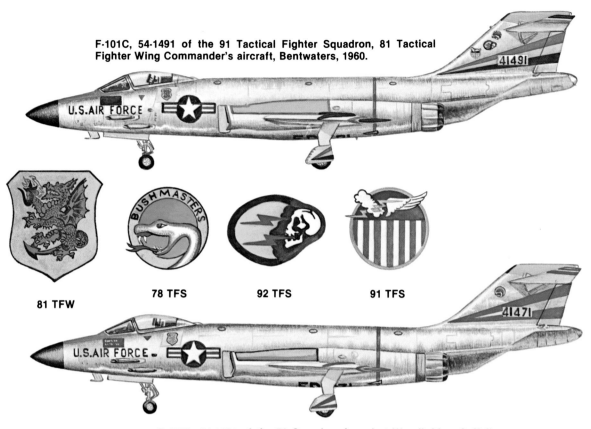

F-101C, 54-1491 of the 91 Tactical Fighter Squadron, 81 Tactical Fighter Wing Commander's aircraft, Bentwaters, 1960.

81 TFW   78 TFS   92 TFS   91 TFS

F-101A, 54-1471 of the 78 Squadron based at Woodbridge, Suffolk, 1960.

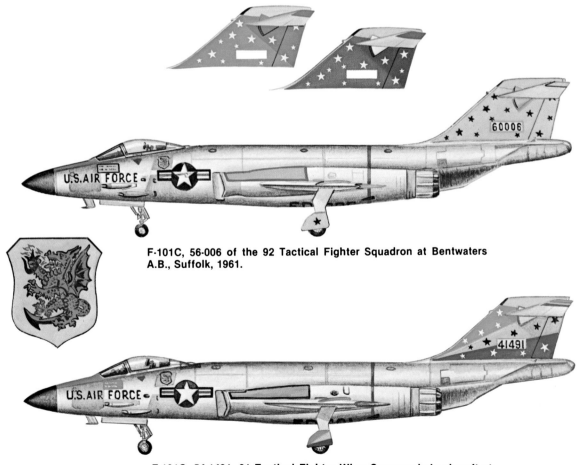

F-101C, 56-006 of the 92 Tactical Fighter Squadron at Bentwaters A.B., Suffolk, 1961.

F-101C, 54-1491, 81 Tactical Fighter Wing Commander's aircraft at Bentwaters A.B., Suffolk, 1961.

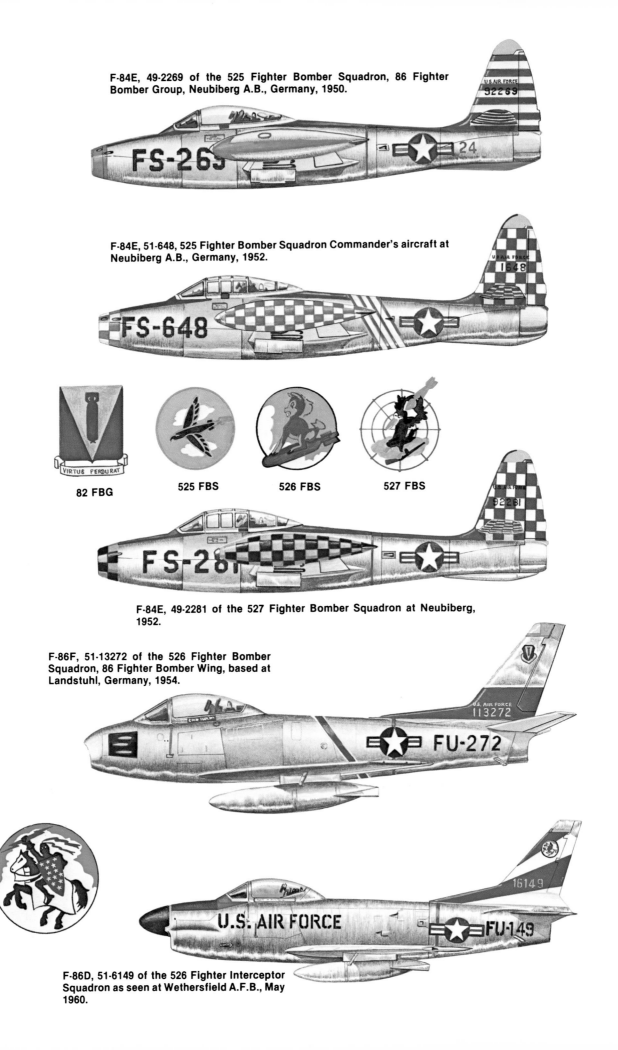

F-84E, 49-2269 of the 525 Fighter Bomber Squadron, 86 Fighter Bomber Group, Neubiberg A.B., Germany, 1950.

F-84E, 51-648, 525 Fighter Bomber Squadron Commander's aircraft at Neubiberg A.B., Germany, 1952.

82 FBG

525 FBS

526 FBS

527 FBS

F-84E, 49-2281 of the 527 Fighter Bomber Squadron at Neubiberg, 1952.

F-86F, 51-13272 of the 526 Fighter Bomber Squadron, 86 Fighter Bomber Wing, based at Landstuhl, Germany, 1954.

F-86D, 51-6149 of the 526 Fighter Interceptor Squadron as seen at Wethersfield A.F.B., May 1960.

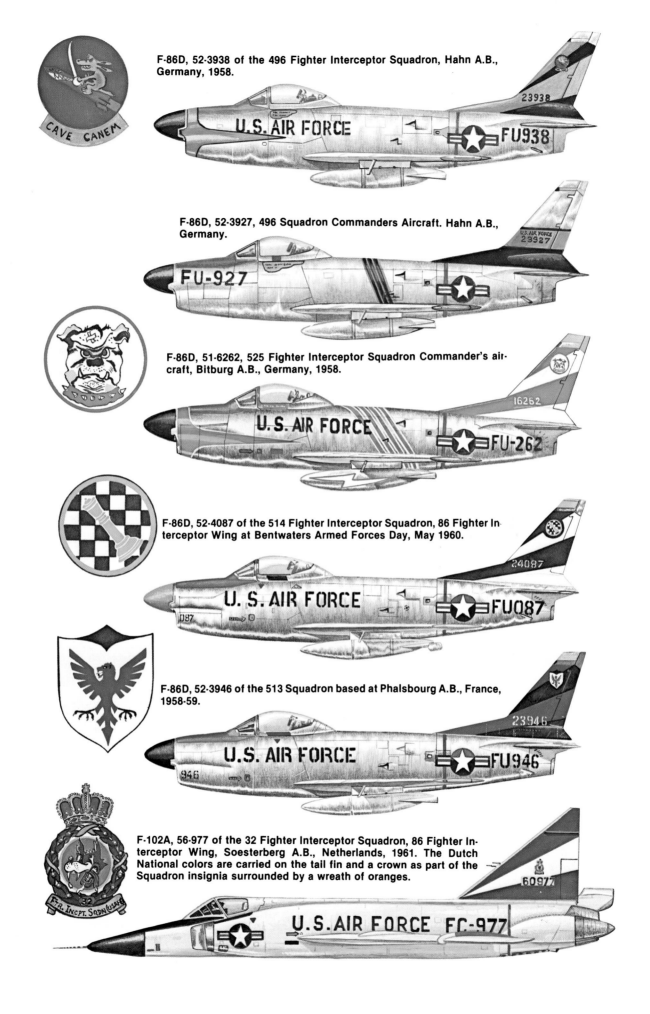

F-86D, 52-3938 of the 496 Fighter Interceptor Squadron, Hahn A.B., Germany, 1958.

F-86D, 52-3927, 496 Squadron Commanders Aircraft. Hahn A.B., Germany.

F-86D, 51-6262, 525 Fighter Interceptor Squadron Commander's aircraft, Bitburg A.B., Germany, 1958.

F-86D, 52-4087 of the 514 Fighter Interceptor Squadron, 86 Fighter Interceptor Wing at Bentwaters Armed Forces Day, May 1960.

F-86D, 52-3946 of the 513 Squadron based at Phalsbourg A.B., France, 1958-59.

F-102A, 56-977 of the 32 Fighter Interceptor Squadron, 86 Fighter Interceptor Wing, Soesterberg A.B., Netherlands, 1961. The Dutch National colors are carried on the tail fin and a crown as part of the Squadron insignia surrounded by a wreath of oranges.

F-102A, 56-1032, 32nd Fighter Interceptor Squadron Commander's aircraft, Soesterberg, 1965. The Squadron color is Green.

F-102A, 54-1405, 496 Fighter Interceptor Squadron Commander's Aircraft, Hahn A.B., Germany, 1961.

F-102A, 56-1080, 496 Fighter Interceptor Squadron Commander's aircraft, Hahn A.B., Germany, 1965.

F-102A, 56-1264, 525 Fighter Interceptor Squadron, 86 Fighter Interceptor Wing, Bitburg A.B., 1961. The aircraft silhouttes contained the pilot's name and the crew chief's name.

F-102A, 56-1044, 525 Fighter Interceptor Squadron Commander's aircraft, Bitburg, 1965. The Air Division insignia was on the right and the Squadron insignia was on the left.

F-102A, 56-1223 of the 526 Squadron *The Black Knights,* **Ramstein A.B., Germany, 1961.**

F-102A, 56-1237 of the 526 Squadron Commander's aircraft, Ramstein A.B., 1965.

F-84E, 51-616 Fighter Bomber Squadron Commander's aircraft, Manston, Kent, 1952.

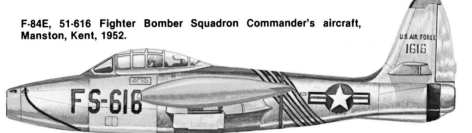

F-86D, 52-10030 of the (Ex.87FIS) 512 Fighter Interceptor Squadron, 406 Fighter Interceptor Wing, Bentwaters, Suffolk, 1956.

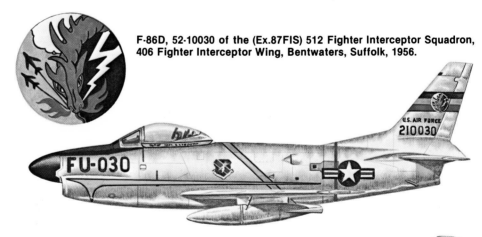

F-86D, 52-4082, 513 Fighter Interceptor Squadron, 406 Fighter Interceptor Wing, seen at Shepherd's Grove A.F.B., Suffolk, May 1957.

F-86D, 52-1009, 514 Fighter Interceptor Squadron Commander's aircraft, based at Manston, Kent, 1957.

F-86D, 52-10012 of the 514 Fighter Interceptor Squadron as seen at Tangmere, September 1957.

F-100C, 55-2720 of the 45 Fighter Day Squadron, based at Sidi Slimane, Franch Morocco, North Africa, 1956.

F-100C, 55-2721 of the 7272 Flying Training Wing at Wheelus A.B., Lybia, 1965.

F-102A, 55-3433 of the 431 Fighter Interceptor Squadron, based at Zaragoza, Spain, 1963.

66th Tactical Reconnaissance Wing
RF-84F Thunderflash

In 1957, the 66th Tactical Reconnaissance Wing comprised four squadrons and operated three types of aircraft.

The aircraft, squadron allocations and colors were as follows:

RF-84F, 302 Squadron - Red
RF-84F, 303 Squadron - Blue
RB-57A, 30 Squadron - Yellow
RB-66   19 Squadron - Blue

The RF-84Fs carried the Squadron colors and star markings on the tail and drop tanks, and the RB-57s had the same application on the tail and wing tip tanks. The RB-66s however, had the markings painted around the jet pod intakes only.

The 66th Wing emblem was positioned on the right side of the nose and Squadron emblem on the left, however, the majority of the aircraft seemed to lack emblems, particularly the Squadron one.

During January 1958, a change in Squadrons took place with the RB-57s and RB-66s being assigned to the 10th Reconnaissance Wing. Their place was taken by the RF-84s of number 32 and 38 Squadrons, both from the 10th Wing. The Yellow markings went to the 32nd squadron while the 38th bore green colors.

66th Tactical Reconnaissance Wing
RF-101C VooDoo

Squadron Colors   *17 TRS Red*   *18 TRS Blue*
32 TRS Yellow   *38 TRS Green*

The latter part of 1958 saw the 66 Wing re-equip with RF-101 Voodoos with the 302 and 303 Squadrons being deactivated. Their place was taken by the 17th and 18th Squadrons carrying red and blue markings respectively, while numbers 32 and 38 retained the yellow and green markings.

The emblems remained in the same applications as on the RF-84s, however, sometimes the N.A.T.O. *Royal Flush* emblem replaced the squadron badge. The *Royal Flush* was an annual event, taking place in Europe each year, whereupon a competition was organized and involved N.A.T.O. reconnaissance squadrons. During this period in the RF-101 markings, the main under carriage wheel doors were painted and in most cases bore an individual letter, possibly to assist with maintenance organization.

By 1961, the individual squadron colors were removed from the tails and replaced by a wide Black band, bordered in White which was edged in Black on all RF-101s. Undercarriage doors were mainly seen in White or Black with appropriate colored letter.

In 1963, colors returned to these RF-101s in the form of a sunburst comprising four colors radiating from a star in a circle. The design being Red, Green, Yellow and Blue (from top to bottom) with White between each color, the star being Yellow on a Blue circular field. Shortly after this, the star motif was replaced by the 66 Wing badge, but the colors remained the same. Markings remained this way until 1965-1966 whereupon camouflage returned.

RF-101C, 56-110 with star on tail, later replaced with the 66th Wing Badge. RAF Wyton, September 1962. (D MENARD)

RF-84F, 52-7343, 303 Tactical Reconnaissance Squadron, 66 Tactical Reconnaissance Wing. Wing Commander's aircraft. Wethersfield AB, 1957. The four fuselage stripes were in the various Squadron colors. (G PENNICK)

RF-101C, 56-211, of the 32 Tactical Reconnaissance Squadron, 66 Tactical Reconnaissance Wing at Hahn AB, Germany. May 1960. (D MENARD)

RF-101C, 56-206 in early 66th Wing Markings. 1961. (USAF)

81 Fighter Interceptor Wing

Squadron Colors   91 FIS   Blue
92 FIS   Yellow   78(ex 116) FIS   Red

In 1951, the F-86A Sabres of the 81 Fighter Interceptor Wing began to arrive into the United Kingdom. The 116 Fighter Interceptor Squadron, was the first to arrive on August 27th at RAF Shepherd's Grove, Suffolk. The 116 had been an Air National Guard Squadron which had been recalled to active duty and assigned to the Wing with its sister squadrons, the 91 and 92 FIS, which followed 116 to the U.K. a month later.

The markings upon arrival consisted of Blue and Orange tail streaks, which later gave way to Blue and Yellow, with fuselage streaks in the individual squadron color with the squadron emblems superimposed on the streaks, these were carried on both sides of the fuselage. Drop tanks on some of the F-86s were also marked with lightning streaks in the appropriate squadron color.

In late 1952, the 116th was re-numbered the 78th FIS, and in 1953, a further change in the markings took place. All colors were replaced by yellow bands, edged in black on the tail and wings for Group markings. Squadron colors were in the form of a band painted around the nose in appropriate color just behind the intake ring and forward of the gun blast panel.

Squadron emblems were sometimes carried on both sides of the fuselage, just below the canopy. A very small *U.S. Air Force* was also to be seen about mid fuselage on both sides.

In October, 1954, 81 Wing began to re-equip with the F-84 Thunderstreak and the Wing title was changed to The 81 Fighter Bomber Wing. Squadrons and colors remained the same with the 78 FBS red, 91 FBS blue, and 92 FBS yellow. The nose design of a band sweeping up and back to the canopy was on all aircraft, the tail markings varied. Very early designs consisted of large factory numbers on the nose sides with squadron emblems on the tail and a single color band below the antenna cover. Later more distinct markings were carried, with the 78 FBS wearing a red sunburst design on the tail, the 91 FBS with a single band below the antenna cover on the tail, and the 92 FBS with a yellow fuselage spine and a solid yellow tail above and below the tail planes. Squadron emblems were carried on both sides of the tail, except for the 92 FBS which carried their badge above the wing and below the rear canopy window for a while. In general, the fuselage badge was that of the 81 FBW on an *Atomic Cloud* superimposed on a light blue winged type motif.

Flight and Squadron Commander's fuselage bands were in evidence particularly with the 78th Bushmasters squadron.

81 Tactical Fighter Wing

July, 1958, saw the unit redesignated 81 Tactical Fighter Wing, and during August of that year, F-101 Voodoos began to arrive at Bentwaters, Suffolk. This was unique as the 81 TFW was the only unit to operate this, the single seat fighter bomber version of the F-101, although the aircraft had previously had a short service with the 27 Fighter Bomber Wing at Bergstrom, Texas, 1957.

Upon arrival at Bentwaters, some of the aircraft sported very colorful markings with their tails painted in the solid squadron color, bearing thirteen stars in appropriate color on each side of the tail and with the wing emblem below the cockpit area on the right side and the squadron emblem on the left side of the cockpit area.

The 81st began removing these markings and by May, 1959, most F-101s were sporting new *sunburst* markings on the tails, main under carriage doors and double bands around the wing tips and horizontal stabilizers. Squadron badges were now placed on both sides of the tail with wing badges on both sides just below the cockpit. F-101C 54-1491 was assigned to the 91 TFS as the 81st Wing Commander's aircraft who at this time was Colonel J.R. Durose. The design was the same as the other F-101s except that triple colors were carried including the three squadron emblems.

Late 1960 and early 1961, saw another change in the markings when the wing reverted to the solid tail colors with star markings as previously used by the 27 TFW, except that now there were additions such as the main under carriage doors being painted in the squadron color with a single star in the center. Wing tips and horizontal stabalizers now carried a wide solid colored band which was trimmed in either white or black depending on Squadron Color.

Squadron Commander's aircraft were also in evidence, such as F-101C 56-0027 of the 92 TFS and had yellow undercarriage doors with four black stars. This particular F-101 was EX 522Sq., 27 TFW and belonged to Major J.J. Burns, who had now become Lt. Colonel and commanded the 92nd.

Another F-101C, 56-0022, bore four white stars on red doors of the 78th TFS, and is believed to be the personal mount of Lt. Colonel P. Stuyvesant then the 78th squadron commander.

The 81 TFW commander's aircraft F-101C 54-1491 now bore the triple colors on the tail, with appropriate colored stars and wing tips, stabalizer tips and main under-carriage doors with triple colors also.

The application of emblems varied somewhat, with aircraft carrying squadron emblems on the left side of the cockpit area, and wing emblems on the right side. Others carried wing emblems on both sides of the cockpit and some carried a single squadron emblem or a solitary wing emblem. However, these markings were some of the most colorful to be seen in Europe and they remained this way until early 1962 when the final change took place. Individual squadron markings were being removed and the triple blue, yellow and red colors were applied to the tails of all aircraft within the 81 Wing with white and black stars respectively. The markings remained this way until 1965 when the Voodoos were returned to the States.

F-86A, 49-1197, 92 F1W seen at Hatfgield 1951-52. Note the crew chief's name on the right canopy frame. (British Aerospace)

(Above) F-84F, 52-6780 of the 78 Fighter Bomber Squadron *Bushmasters*, at its base during an Armed Forces Day celebration. Shepherd's Grove, Suffolk, 1958. (MAP)

(Below) F-101C, 54-1491, 81 Tactical Fighter Wing Commander's aircraft, Bentwaters AFB, Suffolk, 1960. (Via M SUDDS)

F-101C, 56-019, 91 TFS, as seen at Gaydon's Battle of Britain Display, September 1960. (Via M SUDDS)

F-101A, Voodoo, 54-1478 of the 78 Tactical Fighter Squadron *Bushmasters*, based at Woodbridge, Suffolk 1961. (MAP)

F-101C, 56-027 of the 92 Tactical Fighter Squadron, note the four stars on the under carriage doors, believed to indicate the Squadron Commander's aircraft. (D MENARD)

F-101C, 54-1491, 81 Tactical Fighter Wing Commander's aircraft at Bentwaters Armed Forces Day 1961. The tail and landing gear doors are in the Squadrons colors. (D BAKER)

86th Fighter Bomber Group

Squadron Colors   525 FBS   Blue and White
526 FBS   Red and White   527 FBS   Yellow and Black

During 1950, the 86 FBG begun to replace its P-47 Thunderbolts with the F-84Es which had been ferried over by the 27 Fighter Escort Group.

The first markings applied to the F-84s consisted of horizontal red and white striped group markings on all tail surfaces of all the aircraft within the group. Individual squadron markings were applied to the nose and tip tanks in the form of an arrow design on the tip tanks and a band on the intake.

Squadron emblems were carried on both sides of the fuselage above the wing leading edge and squadron commanders and flight leaders carried various numbers of stripes around the fuselage.

In 1951, the markings changes to an even more striking scheme whereby the Group markings consisted of red and white checkers on all tail surfaces with individual squadron colored checkers on the nose intake ring and on the inner and outer side of the tip tanks. The 86th Group emblem was placed on the right side of the fuselage and the squadron on the left, both in the normal positions.

In 1953, the F-86F started to replace the Thunderjets which were sent to Air National Guard Units in the States. Unlike the F-84Es, the markings on the F-86 was comparatively plain with the lower half of the fin and rudder including the dorsal fin being painted in the squadron color. The 525 FBS Blue, 526 FBS Red, and 527 FBS Yellow. The 86 FBW emblem was positioned on both sides of the tail.

Early in 1956, the 527 FBS was redesignated 461 FDS and transferred to the 36th FBW.

In late 1954 and early 1955, the F-86Fs started being replaced by the F-86D interceptor version of the Sabre which arrived via aircraft carrier from the U.S.A. Two new squadrons were also assigned to the **86 Fighter Interceptor Wing** as it was now titled, these being the 440 and 496 FIS.

Markings used on the 525 FIS and 526 FIS are uncertain at the time of this writing. However, the 496 FIS painted the lower quarter of the fin and rudder and dorsal fin in black, with a chrome yellow band just above it, covering another quarter of the fin and rudder. A thin black trim line capped the yellow band, and the *U.S. Air Force* legend and serial were painted in black on the yellow band. About 1956, all 86 FIW Squadrons painted their tails with a sunray with squadron emblems superimposed high on both sides of the tail on the lighter portion of paint. The squadrons and colors were: 440 FIS Orange and Black, 496 FIS Chrome Yellow and Black, 525 FIS medium Blue and White and the 526 FIS Red and White.

In 1958, the 406 FIW based at Manston, Kent de-activated and its three F-86D squadrons were assigned to the 86 FIW at bases in France and Germany. These units adopted new fin markings identical to those already being used by the 86 FIW squadrons. The 513 FIS used Red and Black, the 514 FIS White and Black and it is believed that the 512 FIS adopted a light Yellow and Black so as not to be confused with the 496 FIS. These units also carried their individual squadron emblems on both sides of the tail.

F-86D, 51-028 of the 526 Fighter Interceptor Squadron, 86 Fighter Interceptor Wing. Believed to be the 86th Wing Commander's aircraft with seven fuselage stripes, one for each squadron within the Wing, tail colors are Red and White with the 526 Squadron Badge near the top. Colors of the stripes are unknown. Ramsteim AB, Germany 1958-59.

F-84E, 49-2270, 527 Fighter Bomber Squadron, 86 Fighter Bomber Group, Squadron Commander's aircraft. All markings are Black and Yellow except for Red and White checkered tail. 1952. (Via D MENARD)

F-86D, 52-3899, 513 Fighter Interceptor Squadron, 86 Fighter Interceptor Wing, Alconbury AB, May 1960. (MAP)

86th Fighter Interceptor Wing
F-102A/TF-102 Delta Dagger

During 1959, the F-102A began to appear in Europe, entering service with the 86th Fighter Interceptor Wing, redesignated the 86th Air Division from November 1960.

Four squadrons were to receive the F-102 being numbers 496, 525, 526 and 32, the latter having previously served with the 36th Tactical Fighter Wing, flying F-100Cs.

The color for each of the squadrons were: 496th Yellow and Black, 525th Blue and White, 526th Red and White. The 32nd was Red, White and Blue, however, this particular squadron was still based at Soesterberg in the Netherlands and since it came under dutch control the 32nd carried the colors of the dutch national flag.

The 496th and 525th were first to be equipped with the F-102, the 526th and 32nd following suit in 1960. In the meantime, the 440th, 512th, 513th and 514th squadrons were still operating the F-86D, but by January, 1961, all Sabre Dogs had been de-activated. The markings adopted were similar to those of the F-86Ds with the sunburst sweeping up the tail and the squadron emblems positioned on both sides. The 496 had a new squadron emblem approved in 1960 which contained a clenched fist radiating lightning with a white hooded falcon. The 525th's *Bulldog* emblem changed to brown, while the 32nd was granted permission to place their emblem within the Dutch Crown and a wreath of oranges.

The left side of the F-102s nose had two aircraft silhouettes painted on, one contained the pilot's name and the other was the crew chief's. However, this practice did not extend to the 32nd squadron's aircraft.

All these markings were carried until August 1963, when they were removed from all but a few aircraft. For a while the aircraft remained grey, with only the squadron emblem on the tail. However, by August 1964, new designs were to be seen comprising of a band across the tail with the squadron emblem on the left side and 86th Air Division on the right. At this time the 496th squadron changed from a white to a brown falcon, and the red bomb was deleted from the 86th Air Division emblem since it had long been changed from Fighter Bomber to the Interceptor role.

The 32nd, being the fourth squadron within the wing, bore a green band with the dutch national colors being placed on the speed brakes.

These were the final markings used by all squadrons of the 86th Air Division prior to the advent of camouflage in 1965.

F-86D, 52-3900, with the black and yellow markings of the 440 Fighter Interceptor Squadron, Squadron Commander's aircraft 1958-59. (G JOOS)

F-102A, 56-977, 32 Fighter Interceptor Squadron at Waddington's Battle of Britain Display during September 1961. (MAP)

F-102A, 56-1111, 525 Fighter Interceptor Squadron at Wethersfield's Armed Forces Day in 1961. (MAP)

TF-102A, 54-1366 of the 526 Fighter Interceptor Squadron in full squadron markings. 1961-62 (MAP)

526 Squadron Commander's aircraft in the later style markings, Ramstein, Germany 1965. (MAP)

406 Fighter Bomber Wing

Squadron Colors   512 *Yellow*
513 *Red*   514 *Blue*

The 406th was activated in July 1952, when the called-up Air National Guard wing, the 123rd was re-numbered. The F-84Es being flown by the 123rd were the same aircraft the 31st Fighter Escort Group flew into Manston in January 1951. In August 1951, when the TDY of the 31st was over, the 12th FEG relieved them and took over the aircraft which had been left behind. In early 1952, the 123rd arrived. After being re-numbered, the 123rd squadrons adopted firly simple markings consisting of painting the tip tanks and aircraft noses. The paint on the nose covered the entire intake in a curved design that started at the fuselage top just behind the outboard gun port and swept down and back to a point just behind the nose gear well, covering the nose gear doors almost completely with the color being used.

The *flight assigned within the squadron* colors were carried in a band completely around the extreme rear of the fuselage, just under the elevators. No fin markings appear to have been carried, and the buzz numbers on the noses were not the factory applied ones. The 512th used Yellow for its color while the 513th used Red and the 514th used Blue.

406 Fighter Bomber Group

During 1953, the F-86F started to replace the F-84E.

Group markings consisting of a triple colored band of light Blue, Yellow and Red with then Black trim lines, was painted diagonally across the aircraft tails. Individual squadron color, which remained the same, was placed just behind the intake ring.

In November 1954, the 512 FBS was transferred to Soesterberg in the Netherlands and redesignated the 32 Fighter Day Squadron in

September 1955. At this time the 512 squadron number returned to Bentwaters in suffolk, taking over the F-86D aircraft, insignia and mission of the 87 FIS whose squadron number was returned to the U.S.A. The 512 squadron now joined the 406th Group again, and together with the other two squadrons still assigned, the 513 and 514 FBS, during late 1954 was redesignated 406 Fighter Interceptor Wing and the whole unit commenced flying the F-86D Sabre Dog.

Markings on the tails remained the same with the triple colored diagonal tail band, but had the individual squadron emblems applied to the middle of both sides. The individual squadron colors took the form of a lightning flash placed low on the fuselage just behind the intake. Canopy frames also carried the squadron color.

A short time later, the Blue, Yellow and Red tail bands were placed horizontally across the tail, still retaining the squadron emblems. Canopy sills were now painted in squadron colors on both sides and a stylized 'harpoon' was painted on the lower portion of the fuselage in squadron colors. Various forms of squadron commander's and flight leaders fuselage bands were applied and the 512 FIS was known to have carried the wing emblem on the fuselage sides at one stage in its history.

In 1958, the 406 FIW was deactivated and its three squadrons were assigned to the 86 FIW. The markings completely changed and the 86 FIW style was adopted. The 512 FIS at Sembach A.B., Germany, carried light Yellow and Black, the 513 FIS at Phalsborg, France Red and Black and finally, the 514 FIS at Ramstein, Germany with White and Black.

All three units finally deactivated in late 1959 and in 1960.

F-86D, 52-10110 with very striking markings of the 512 Fighter Interceptor Squadron, 406 Fighter Interceptor Wing, Burtonwood Armed Forces Day, 1958. (D MENARD)

F-86D, 51-6188, 514 Fighter Interceptor Squadron based at Manston, Kent. 1957.

431 Fighter Interceptor Squadron

The 7272 FTW's operations group at Wheelus A.B., Libya contained a number of constituent units, one of which worked towards providing effective air defence of the Libyan area. This was the 431 FIS based at Wheelus from 1953, operating the F-86D Sabre.

The markings were rather unique and very striking, consisting of White outlined 'Satans Heads' with a Yellow winged 'Halo' and five Yellow stars forming the southern cross, all was on a broad dark Red band with white and blue trim lines.

Around 1958, the 431st moved to Zaragoza A.B., Spain and in 1960, began to convert to the F-102, so the 'Satan' design was transferred to the tail of this aircraft. The TF-102s carried the markings in greater depth, in fact, parallel with the top of the speed brakes with the unit citation and serial number below.

These markings were carried through to 1965.

45 Fighter Day Squadron

The 45 Fighter Day Squadron was stationed in French Morocco from mid 1953 until early 1958. Their original aircraft were F-86F, but in 1956, F-100Cs replaced them. The 45th then became the transition unit for USAFE fighter pilots transitioning from the F-84s and F-86 to the F-100. Markings carried on their F-86 Sabres are unknown at the time of writing, but their Super Sabre markings were rather unique. These consisted of a wide yellow diagonal band across the middle third of the fin, with two highly stylized black and yellow "check marks" forming the top and bottom borders of the band. The yellow was also used on a scalloped band around the intake. When drop tanks were carried, the fins were yellow with a scalloped intake design on the forward portion of the tank, but not including the nose of the tank. The 45th briefly flew F-100Ds, but it is not known if the yellow markings were applied to these models.

7272 Flying Training Wing

The 7272 Flying Training Wing was tasked with the training and evaluation of european based fighter squadrons and was based at Wheelus in Lybia. Aircraft operated included the T-33A, B-57E, F-100C and F-100F, with one of their jobs being target towing.

In the late 1950s and early 60s, the F-100C markings consisted of a red tapered band across the tail with yellow trim. The band commencing with a point from the dorsal fin, sweeping up and back, ending with a wide portion at the top rear end of the tail. The nose intake was also red with a yellow trim line.

During 1962, these markings were removed and the Wing badge was placed on both sides of the tail. However, 1964 saw the return of very smart dark blue and white markings on all of the 7272 FTW aircraft and they remained this way until deactivated some years later.

F-100C, 55-2721, 7272 FTW at Lakenheath AB, Suffolk 1965. (MAP)

F-102A, 55-3450 of the 431 Fighter Interceptor Squadron with the Devils Head on tail which was taken from their Squadron Emblem. C1963-64. (MAP)